When We Think of Mama

By Coleen
everglades Lewis

Illustrated by
Alyssa Lasko

When We Think of Mama

Hardcover ISBN 978-1-7345570-7-7
Paperback ISBN 978-1-7345570-8-4
eBook ISBN 978-1-7345570-9-1

Written by Coleen Everglades Lewis
Illustrated by Alyssa Lasko

Patty Spoonbill
BOOKS

A mother is a light that shines in spaces dark and bright.
She is the beautiful soul that gives comfort to all.
Whether your mother is alive
or resting in peace, always remember:
she is a radiant sunflower,
forever graceful, forever strong, forever in our hearts.

Coleen Everglades
Lewis Author

Love you mommy

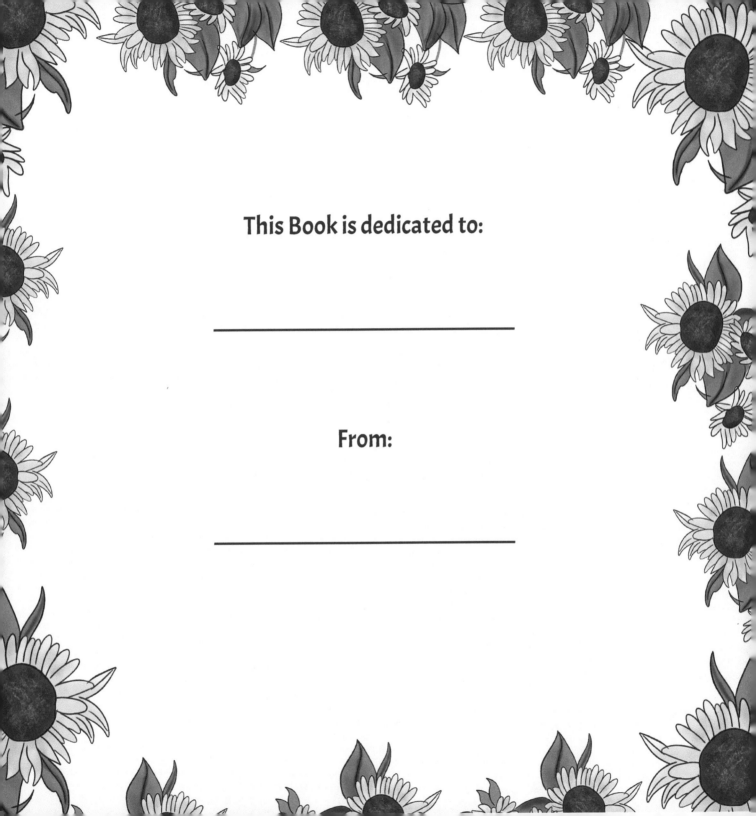

This Book is dedicated to:

_____

From:

_____

Sunrays
warm and golden
like honeycomb,
dancing off Mama's hair at noonday
as she plants her sunflowers.

Mama makes the world our home.

Sun-kissed sunflowers
filled with precious memories
of seashells mixed in sea sand,
sea gulls and sea grapes,
sea turtles paddling to the seashore,
and Mama's full lips when she smiles.

Manman makes the world our home.
(Haiti-Creole)

Native sunflowers
a halo of light facing the sun,
because light knows light,
and beauty follows beauty,
of which you are both,
like Mama,
the heartbeat of our people.

Mother makes the world our home.

Radiant sunflowers
golden petals dipped in gold,
a jewel to behold,
like Mama's soft skin,
as she cradles me to bed
after a long day of play.

Ang aking Ina makes the world our home.

(Philippine)

Divine sunflowers
timeless as planets circling the sun,
pure as crisp air skating across the sky,
beautiful as the rainbow tucked in the clouds,
precious as Mama's love for her children.

Amma makes the world our home.
(India)

Blooming sunflowers
sprinkles of morning dew and sunrays
makes you tall and strong.
When Mama cuddles me in her arms and
says it's okay to cry,
be happy,
or just be me,
regardless of what others may say,
I grow tall and strong.

Ibu makes the world our home.
(Indonesia)

Majestic sunflowers
a gift from Mother Earth,
beloved children of the sun, moon, and stars,
roots planted deep and firm,
like Mama's brave words,
"Precious child, love yourself."

Vieja makes the world our home.
(Spanish)

Heavenly sunflowers
swaying under the sun,
tap, tapping to the beat of steel drums.
Music so rhythmic and pure
it reminds me of Mama's heart,
blooming with love and hope
for all children.

Mooma makes the world our home.
(Trinidad)

Long-stemmed sunflowers
magical fairies under a half moon,
when I drift off to sleep,
you color my dreams,
with sprinkles of wildflowers and spring flowers,
dragonflies and fireflies,
cat tales and puppy tales,
and Mama's soulful eyes
when they crinkle with joy.

Mère make the world our home.
(Canada-French Canadian)

Beloved sunflowers
like stars,
like dinosaurs,
like our ancestors,
all things die.
Although we are sad they are gone,
their memories live in our hearts.

Ima makes the world our home.
(Israel-Hebrew)

Our hearts glow like sunflowers
when we think of Mama.

Mama makes the world our home.

Mother in different languages:

American/Caribbean: mama, ma, mom, mommy, madda, mother
Albanian: nënë
Arabic: أمي ,'um, mum, mama, mummy, mammy
Canada (French Canadian): mère
Czech: matka
Chinese: 妈妈
Danish: mor
Dutch: moeder
England: mum, mom

French: méré
German: mutter
Ghana: bamama
Greek: untépa,
Haiti: manman
Hawaii: makuahine
Hindi: माँ, Mãm, mum, mama, ma,
momma, mummy
Hungarian: anya
India: Amma, mathaji

Indonesia: Ibu
Irish: Máthair
Israel (Hebrew): Ima
Italian: madre
Japanese: 母
Kenya: madha, Mrs.
Latin: matr, mater
Nigeria: mommy (then attach the name of their children behind the word-mommy Kanele etc.)
Norwegian: mamma, mor
Pakistan: ماں
Polish: mama

Phillippines: ina, nanay, inang
Portuguese: mãe
Russian: matb
Somalia: hooyo
South Africa: bamama
Spanish: madré
Tiawan: muqin
Ukraine: мати
Welch: mam
Zimbabwe: Amai, mama